X : POEMS

poems by

James Galvin

COPPER CANYON PRESS

Cover art: Calligraphy by Glen Epstein

Copper Canyon Press is in residence under the auspices of
the Centrum Foundation at Fort Worden State Park in Port Townsend,
Washington. Centrum sponsors artist residencies, education workshops for
Washington State students and teachers, Blues, Jazz, and Fiddle Tunes
festivals, classical music performances, and
the Port Townsend Writers' Conference.

LIBRARY OF CONGRESS CATALOGING-IN-PUBLICATION DATA

Galvin, James.
X : poems / by James Galvin. — 1st ed.
p.   cm.
ISBN 1-55659-191-8 (alk. paper)
I. Title.   PS3557.A444X17 2003
811'.54 — dc21   2002154675

COPPER CANYON PRESS
Post Office Box 271
Port Townsend, Washington 98368
www.coppercanyonpress.org

Acknowledgments

Thanks to the magazines in which some of these poems
first appeared: *AGNI, Boston Review, Denver Quarterly, DoubleTake, Fence,
The New Yorker, Orion, Seneca Review, TriQuarterly,* and *Volt.*

CONTENTS

— I —

E quella a me: «Nessun maggior dolore
    che ricordarsi del tempo felice
    nella miseria; e ciò sa 'l tuo dottore.»

LITTLE DANTESQUE

It turns out
The dogs were in control all along.

Hard by the hinges of Hell —
A faculty party.

Everyone drifts
In their disastrous bodies.

Sudden furniture,
A hint of eucalyptus.

Someone plugs in the flowers.

1

I've been a has-been.
Now I'm a was. I was
Promoted.

2

The dogs were in control all along.
They saw everything.

3

I had a happy medium —
Had her reading out of my palm.
The circus folded up and left —

A riot of life-forms
And annoying colors whisked
Like bright scarves up a sleeve.

4

The dogs want out.
How like them.

DEAR MAY EIGHTH

Why was the last kiss May seventh
And so shy?

Your tongue was skittish.

Your clavicle —
Door-bolt, little key,
Tendril —
Was the world's crosstree —
Your collarbone was hot snow to touch.

I wanted to say commitment,
And so I was committed,
And so I did commit
Crimes against the immaculate.

Clavicle, clavichord,
Gold keys falling through me cold.

You explain
The sky I spent my life under,
The bottom of the ocean
That packed up and left.

You say it's the basin that makes the sky a bay.

The sunset plans its palette, its deployment.

It hasn't decided the denouement —
It's breathless....

Listen, Nobody's Business,
Why aren't you in love with me?

Is your overture over-subtle
Like this sunset —
White clavicle under gray thunderheads,
Cobalt throbs?

Streaky northern billows
And reds thrum into music — clavichord.

Then — get this —
Red cliff
Is palindromed,
Butterflied, flayed,
In strata of lenticulars.

Rain rains down
Blue-black on earth
And sends riders, striders,
Bruisy yellow,
Blood in a stream,
Back to the eastern horizon —
Where I kissed you.

If you would wake with me
I'd know how to die.

Yours, May eighth,
Sincerely,
Man under influence of sky.

DEAR NOBODY'S BUSINESS

What did you expect
Threadbare me to do
With nothing to deflect
The gale of your remove?

The scanty sacred secret
Tries to thumb a ride
Through drubbed, irresolute,
And famously slippery light.

Like a spooky spark from an anvil
The sun makes a teary streak
Across the almost tranquil,
Which is the almost bleak.

What is threadbare me to do
When wind cleaves your summer dress
To almost all of you?

WILD IRISES ON DIRTY WOMAN CREEK

Stars leak mixed feelings
Over sheet lightning's weft of echoes.
You, I can't get over your shoulder blades,
Like music from the center of the earth.
I want to live happily.
You can have the ever and the after.
You are quite lifelike, but you can't fool me.
I know the unearthly when I die from it.
I'm not talking about the body's mutable components —
I'm not talking.
Look — wild irises, like every spring,
In the salacious green of Dirty Woman Creek.

ALPENROSE GROWING BY THE DOOR

Bride of the desert
Dawdling in eternity, fully
In the sight of God,
Rampant stupor,
If it rains get in it
With your luteous lower leaves.
Where are we? What dream brought us?
Singsong splinterings jut into twilight.
Shadows we are, inclined to refusal,
Refusing, for example, to cast shame
On the firelight of burning villages,
Our visages smudged, bewildered, kind.
Oh wretched road in rain,
The only road that goes where we go,
Me without you — you, yet, with me.
Aren't you ashamed?
Your sustenance is refusal, and who's to say
It serves you ill?
Well, think fondly of me, gone as you drift
Into your heaven of hesitation.
I loved you, alpenrose.
I was your daredevil problem child,
Just here to amuse you with vain attempts
At rising up out of death.

ROLLING SUN

While that lucky old sun has nothin' to do
But roll around heaven all day.

I bear a ghost to the lost
Like an ant carrying a butterfly.
I think the world of ashes.
I think the world of sky.
Velocities and trestletrees
Will take you
To a paradise of suffering.
One apocalypse deserves another, no?
The bonds are binding.
Inertia cleaves.
No frills.
Kiss me.

SHOW-AND-TELL

This is the wave of gravel where she let me off on the edge of my life.
    This is the gleaming edge, past agencies and scrap.
                              This is the
edge of a blighted field where God idles his tractor.
                           He thinks he's a
thunderhead in drought.
               You think God doesn't have a tractor?
                                  You
think he doesn't have a blighted field?
                  This is what he's thinking:
not yet, not yet.
        Look, there's another panic button lying on the
ground.
      Look, here comes another wave of gravel.
                      Look, here
comes night.
       You think God can't give up?

PREVAILING WIND

Without inherent power to exist,
Attempting bravely to preserve some form,
Leaning into your confidence like pure
Time with nothing in it, giving deeper
Draft to stars' keels, you stop, and the night
Leaves hang like phials of morphine. Inept ecstasy,
Ecstatic inanity, despondent, burning
Splendor, prevailing wind, prevailing modest
And hushed, paying strict attention while
Reviling thunder. A yellow aspen, caught
In a whirling updraft you didn't think about,
Sketches you, your portrait, capturing
You perfectly, with ease, your hurricane
Mane swirling as you pass without passing.

FIRE SEASON

All the angels of Tie Siding were on fire.

The famous sky was gone.

Presumably the mountains were still there, invisible in haze.

OK,
there was only one angel, but she was a torch in the wind, beside
the wind-ripped American flag the post office flies.

OK, she wasn't
literally on fire.

Maybe her angelic red hair made me think she was
ablaze as it flaunted the prairie and made a festival of itself.

There
was a fireworks stand nearby, entirely beside the point, as was the
Fourth of July.

It was really dry.

It was fire season.

It was the
wind festival, featuring an angel standing in it, letting her red hair
conflagrate history, reduce it to ash, bid it start anew, erase the sky
with atrocity's own smoke.

She wore, besides her flame of hair,
blue jeans and a singlet.

She was violent in the wind.

I started
walking toward her.

I'm still walking toward her, no idea what to
say when I get there.

PONDEROSA

It was out in the middle of the light, no way back for that old giant.

Other trees stood cloaked at a safe distance.
I used to think its
name meant it was thoughtful.
It did look like a green brain on a
stem, alive in wind.
I thought it got emotions from its roots in
earth, intelligence from needles in the sun.
I thought it must make
sense of everything.
Basque shepherds carved their love poems in
its bark and cut Lascaux-like glyphs of antelope and girls.
Those
Basques — Matisses of the plains, gouging desires into a thinking
tree that seemed to come striding over the horizon, like a verdant
thunderhead, mushroom cloud of true benignity.
Sooner or later, we
all knew, lightning had to strike, and when it did we saw it.
The bolt
came down like knowledge, but the tree did not explode or burn.
It
caught the jolt and trapped it like a mythic girl.
Its trunk was three
feet through.
Lightning couldn't blow the ponderosa into splinters,
and couldn't burn inside without some air.
A week went by and we

forgot about it.

         But lightning is a very hot and radiant girl.

                       When
heat bled out to bark, the tree burst into flame that reared into
silence under a cloudless sky.

           Brain of ash, what can you tell me
now?

    What were your thoughts, concerning history?

EARTHQUAKE

A well-dressed mannequin with a price tag on her sleeve — what
could be closer to the truth, unless an earthquake rocks her lifelike.

A woman eating an orange in an earthquake — what could be closer
to the truth?
        The luminescent globe perches on four of her
fingertips, which are the four definitions of beauty.
                The earthquake
is self-conscious because it means no harm.
                I am waiting for my
life to be over because it couldn't be closer to the truth.
                Here's
what the earthquake feels like: something you'd like to step off of,
please, onto something else, but can't.
                The exoskeletons of survival
strategies are strewn over the plain.
                They are the most beautiful
airports.
    I've read a lot of books in which all the protagonists had to
do was say something true, and everything would turn out all right,
a comforting twilight.
                They never do.
                Without fail they fall
unchecked into a comfortable misery.
                The woman eats the orange,
segment by segment, longitude by longitude.
                She separates segment
from segment, as if there were truth in an orange.
                She could take

forever.

Each time she peels another glowing crescent it sounds like
the turning of a page.

The earthquake is just descant.

The ground
undulates — so what.

She perches the light-lusty globe on her
fingertips and pulls it apart like pages agonized into a story where
nothing could be closer to the truth.

The truth?

Fault and slip,
broken limbs, swooning buildings, an inner din unending.

SO LONG

I look down at my hand and there's a wrinkling ocean in it.
A halcyon nest rocks on careless waves.
Small in the bottom of the nest, fledgling, my father curls.
He doesn't look so good.
What I say, what he says, what does it matter?
I've got this ocean in my hand, and there's no cure for that.

DYING INTO WHAT I'VE DONE

True to the past because
Only the past is true,
I am not required to cover up
The blunders of whimpering windows,
Luminously weak
From their odd liquidity —
Lanky hair when it rains,
Obscure convictions of night,
A vague but towering,
A nameless, swaying urge,
Arrant nonsense.
There has to be something still
At the center of the swirl —
Ask any hurricane —
An *everlasting,* an *all-powerful,*
A *Let's grow old together and die*
In each other's arms —
Or the one left back dies soon of grief everlasting,
A *no-matter-what.*
Else the swirl cannot be
More than a stillborn breeze.
Something has to be true enough to be
Taken for granted.
In the hospital I saw
An old man
Caressing the face of an old woman.
This same man, young, caressed her face
In just that way.
That's the stillness

At the center of change —
A sadness worth dying for, I swear —
There is no other.
Going it alone,
Cloistered and spectral,
Glozed over by a weeping god,
Meet my new bride:
The air I breathe —
A never fixèd mark.
I walk backwards into the sun.
I feel its heat on my shoulders.
We stroll together like backward lovers.
The eye of the storm without the storm
Is not death.
It is the embodiment of death.

LIMBER PINES

Limber pines are the suicide trees, nothing holding back their
sensibilities, and nothing to make them say what it is they feel as
they rush into clearings like people fleeing a movie house in flames
or jumping from a sundered ship into a burning sea.

Their weakness
is their ability to take hold anywhere.

Their strength is their ability
to die.

They are the bark beetle's favorite lunch, the wildfire's
favorite witch, the wind's best game of dominoes.

Sometimes you
see one clinging to a sunwashed rock, like the castaway a little later,
but limber pines can squeeze blood from a stone and drink it.

Their
roots crack granite, hold, live on next to nothing and, stunted, grow
into wizened children.

PROMISES ARE FOR LIARS

Because, you know,
Either you're going
To do it or
You're not.
Slight as light
Reflected from the stream
Onto the wavering
Willow leaves,
Eternal love
Doesn't need
Eternity, see?
A cyclone of sand-
Hill cranes
Rises from the corn
Slathering the
Ephemeral work.
Let's don't worry.
Let's don't ask.
Our institutions
Are standing by.
But I keep thinking
How easy it is
To get lost in the sky
With nothing holy
To defend.

BAD SAMARITANS

Most Samaritans, of course, are Bad,
Otherwise there wouldn't be a story
Or way to explain the alarm the Man-Fallen-
Among-Thieves expresses on being offered
An unknown, viscous, bitter panacea,
Or why the Samaritan himself recoils
To see his generosity reviled.
A Good Samaritan refused is no
More good than any Bad Samaritan,
Any Samaritan born to be Bad,
One of a den of thieves to fall among
As into a large field of black poppies.
Of course the story works things out for us,
Whereas in real life the Man-Fallen-
Among-Thieves just bleeds and bleeds, while the fields
Of black poppies flee to the night horizon.

OUGHT

A feud unites
Math and myth.
A feud cleaves
Quiddity and quiddity.
The tryst is *triste*,
A slipknot.

A mendicant hoaxes
The suzerain.
The feal paladin
Follows his dame,
Is damned, loose
As ashes, his ambit is

Loose as ashes.
Loss, his love,
Is a bucket of nerves.
Algorithmic,
Epigenetic,
He ciphers ciphers.

He transfigures
Liquid dynamics:
Earthy to unearthly.
His lore distinguishes
Amenable secrets
(Amen), extinguishes

Feudal dander.
He sunders ought.
I ought to write
The end of this
Mass of math,
This mess with
Life is lief.

JET STREAM

Who doubts the existence of the jet stream, traceable only by the
martyrs of meteorology, as it oscillates within its limits?

When the
weather it engenders interrupts our psychic flow, injury, inevitable,
ensues.

This has nothing to do with anything but love.

The
constant and the variant need each other to know who they are, to
kiss.

Hordes of tenacious seconds turn to years.

Just because I tell
the truth is no reason to trust me.

Don't trust me.

I'm just another
humanitarian disaster.

Attempts at rescue only made me worse.

Great would be the wonder of the gods, but they don't wonder.

Tites and mites — you know — the stalag sisters — live in caves and
pass the time and sometimes meet.

Calamity flows.

We weather,
unlike gods.

Marooned on a shred of wind, I say my say.

In the
upper troposphere, in the lower stratosphere, the jet stream
screams, invisible because made of air, up to one hundred fifty
miles per hour, a shiftless paradigm, a cat's tail twitch.

Down here,

under the weather, a fine fall day, switch and twitch are not responsible for these trees turning to fire, not responsible for the heaps we make from what they let go.

I fell asleep this afternoon to the shouts of children falling into leaves.

DOUBLE RAINBOW

Well aren't you the harsh necessity,
As in what fear is for?
It was the summer of
You should have been there,
Though the last thing I want
Anywhere near me is you.
Louche and thaumaturgic,
You made my faith
My foolishness —
Easy as lying to trees.
Essence of the inessential
Is what you are, double rainbow,
Extrinsic as blood is to stars,
An empire not of death,
But inspired by death,
Farrago of arid precepts,
A few cheap ideas about hope,
The eschaton, alterity,
All featuring you.
What are the chances?
Slim to none.
But listen here, my fraud, my forger,
I could close my eyes at any time.
All I have to do is close my eyes.

UPSLOPE

To say that you exaggerate would be an understatement.
Cars lick the rainslick street.
Author, authority,
Master, mastery,
If I wear glasses am I more spectacular?
Tweezer-brain causality.
When you left
I woke, and it was my whole life I woke from.
Upslope, geography offers history few options.
We are something's awareness,
Awareness of fog, for instance.
God saves us in the sorrow of knowing him.

CONFLAGRATION OF OPPOSITES

Over the summer, unbeknownst,
Barn swallows built a grass and twig nest
Tight as a hay bale, tobacco plug,
In the chimney top.
When the first Arctic air snugged
Down, itself a cradle for winter,
I lit the hearth fire and smoke
Breech-birthed, a black snow of soot
Over the furniture.

So out of love with life am I
No future will have me.
How can you lose a lie?
Well, you can. Easy.
All those years together, it seems,
Were posturings of goodbye.
For a time I raved.
Now I dwell in moods and reveries
Like frighted birds —

Vacant panic, raging desolation —
Not the living forest on fire, but after,
Green boughs burnt to a fare-thee-well.
The bark and squeak of a windmill,
Windwell, no help now,
Says I told you so, whippersnapper,
Whisper ripped in air.
I love you so much I don't know who you are,
Demolition derby, sauntering abattoir.

Your entitlement comes from the mirror,
Your confidence smolders.
It was the truth that did it, yes,
And it was the lies.
Extremophile, you lied to everyone,
Lies with wings.
When history was invented,
Evil ceased to be the enemy.
That's your no-fault policy.

Now I don't care what you do.
I've seen your worst at its best.
Did I fall through a trapdoor in the sky?
Swallows rose from the chimney.
You are in love with someone else.
I saw the adoration in your eyes
Like burning nests,
Like Buddhists in flame,
Rocking, lifting black wrists.

FREEZING RAIN

Restraint and shame are pretty much the same, unless restraint is shameless cowardice, which doesn't count.

We're cruelest to those we love the most, who don't expect it.

Don't let on how much you have forsaken.

Freezing rain says, *Face the music.*

Freezing rain says, *I mean it.*

Think of a pretty girl in a black bath.

Oh, she's sitting pretty in her black bath.

Theories advocating incapacity snake through art.

Through and through until they're through.

How do I start over now, having been wrong about everything?

Being has no beginning, so leave me alone.

Winds are muscles, aren't they.

Face the music.

Don't let on about what made us *want* to live.

Let freezing rain bear witness for a change.

HEAT WAVES IN WINTER DISTANCE

Cloud brow over the swaying Medicine Bow,
These thoughts of mine — they're yours.
Pray for me as I pray
For you to turn tacit,
To cauterize me in a searing kiss.
You know — I know you know —
Just how much blood is out there,
Most of it in circulation,
Enough to make a single drop worthless.
Mark my words.
Imagine an anorexic mosquito,
Euphemistic as the number two,
Hot all over.
Dried blood is not worth anything either,
Except to the awful law
That turns against
Its former mirror image ripped in waves,
Electrified by heat in distance.
My mother waved goodbye
Every single day I left for school.
Heat waves, particle waves, tidal waves —
You know.

RIVER EDGED WITH ICE

The truest friend of all is in the earth
With you, rattletrap, but it isn't you.
The friend I mean knows neither back nor forth.

You're all talk, light, and dissolute sweetness.
Houses gaze on you reflectively,
But the truest friend of all is in the earth.

Immured in glaze, impartial as all get-out,
But never neutral, you know what I'm saying.
The friend I mean knows neither back nor forth.

...Intoxicated by celebrity,
Indifferent as the moon to your destiny....
The truest friend of all is in the earth

Like you are, but the truest friend is still,
Completely still, still as a frozen lake.
The friend I mean knows neither forth nor back.

You bear your own destiny away,
More ardent, less compassionate than she.
The one I love flows neither back nor forth.
The truest friend of all is in the earth.

WINTER SOLSTICE FULL MOON AT PERIGEE

Being in love isn't about being happy.
Here's a good idea: let's live some more.

After bad things happen we always live
A little more. Good timing, bad timing,

The people against me were probably right:
You can't step in front of the same bus twice.

From here on out, honesty's its own
Intelligence, which may or may not involve

Philosophy. Try to understand
The world, and leave the mind to darkness where

It thrives. Werner Herzog, for example, says
The mind is a room, better dimly lit

For livable ambience, some lively music
For habitability — than floodlit, mute

For self-knowledge — a bogus notion, anyway.
According to the quarterback from Cedar

Rapids, Iowa, Jesus is a
Football fan, without whose intervention

The Rams could not have won the Super Bowl.
Aren't you ashamed at refusing love

Like an hors d'oeuvre (*outside the work* — which was?).
Love's not love until it's lost, and then

You write a corybantic poem about it.
That's what you think. What I think — what do I think?

I think the house we lived in wept itself
All the way down. I think forgiveness mirrors

Facetious animals at play: horseplay.
Horse sense, more what we aspire to —

Remains the province of the horses, no?

JANUARY THAW

Winter snowpack is not your jazz.
You can't riff it over and you can't take it back
Once it's out of the horn.
Bright as tears but much more boring,
Your constants without variants
Mewl from the eaves.
That's why the fish is full of sea.
Just out of curiosity,
How many times did you kiss me
Without meaning it?
Don't be shy, it's out of the horn.
Turn your back on the past
And you're gone.

LEAP YEAR

When the river goes underground it isn't lying.

I used to have

someone to miss.

Forgetting about the future makes the moment
you live in slouch.

Excuse me while I digest this small galaxy.

In

a petri dish of hubris, fear and sorrow are exculpatory and lead to
an event-free life.

The waterfall fell and the river went

underground.

Terror is transvertebrated to attraction, making you

feel more godly.

Quite a leap.

The river went to hell.

The waterfall

fell.

Down here we don't have moods.

Nothing amounts to

anything.

The man with a fishhook in his eye can see quite clearly.

The rain never comes, but dry lightning in a thunderhead is like
cotton candy being electrocuted.

When the river comes back up

again we call it spring.

Oh, Persephone, home's not where I

thought it was.

Home is where the heart gives out and we arouse

the grass.

SHOW ME YOUR ORIGINAL FACE, THE FACE YOU HAD BEFORE YOUR PARENTS WERE BORN

My soul is unemployed.
I am stronger than death.
A tyranny of fire escapes attacks the facades.
Here on the abyssal plain the wind is made of water,
But weather is the same,
As is the cost of living.
Underwater horses graze in underwater sage.
I am their sagesweet horsesmell.
The silence is too beautiful to break.
Look, I am the immaculate conception.

CHERRY BLOSSOMS BLOWING IN WET, BLOWING SNOW

In all the farewells in all the airports in all the profane dawns.

In the Fiat with no documents on the road to Madrid.
                                              At the
corrida.
            In the Lope de Vega, the Annalena, the Jerome.
                                                    In time
past, time lost, time yet to pass.
                        In poetry.
                                    In watery deserts, on
arid seas, between deserts and seas.
                            In sickness and in health.
                                                    In
pain and in the celebration of pain.
                            In the delivery room.
                                                In the
garden.
            In the hammock under the aspen.
                                    In all the emergencies.
                                                        In
the waterfall.
            In toleration.
                        In retaliation.
                                    In rhyme.
                                            Among cherry
blossoms blowing in wet, blowing snow, weren't we something?

NATURE, BESIDE HERSELF

Nothing is at one with nature,
Not wind or wind-tried trees,
Not striving grass,
Not famished coyotes or lovesick whales.
How do I know?
Interviews.
Without the part
Where I point out the obvious —
The *not with us* — there's no such thing as nature,
Is there?
It's just another everywhere where
We loiter
Outside in order
To side-glance in.

SUNSET THROUGH
SPRING SNOW

Grave warmth,
Someone else's
Life becomes mine.
Pray for me.

Somewhere a star
Gutters out,
A fleet of balloons
Comes to grief.

How long
Is as long as I want?
Large units
Of time, I'll tell you

That, catapulted
Toward outcome
Such as a sloop
In its slip

Bursting into flame.
Such as knuckles
Sore from knocking,
The voice inside rasping,

No more Mozart for you!
Fear makes me
Want you more.
Shall we go to our graves

Without knowing,
Or would we rather die
Of what we know?
I fear your reluctance

In regard to the ineluctable
Singularity.
I was sublime,
Subliming, sublimated,

Extinguished —
Charming as a bee in amber,
Having seized in pitch,
Foundered, mired,

Crucified into artifact.
Some clouds are beating
Up some other clouds —
Oh, bloody tresses.

DEPENDING ON THE WIND

1

A score of years ago I felled a hundred pines to build a house.

Two stories, seven rooms in all.
                        I built my love a home.
                                         Our
daughter was in orbit in the womb.
                             Mountains spun off like the arm
of a galaxy into the emptiness our windows framed.
                               "What a
view!" our friends exclaimed, and "Sunsets to die for every single
night!"

2

Vertigo of solitude, distillate of loneliness for blood, my wife
untrue, my daughter flown, I, like a widower or worse, move
among the rooms I made.
                        Where once I was not alone, now each
closed door is panic, and spaces grow immense with memory, like
shadows at dusk.
                  Gone that arrangement of allegiances called *family*
we never really know before it ends.
                          Like love itself, it isn't true till
then.
    I have no family now but remembrances of tiny joys, tinier
dramas we used to call *our life*, like pollen over everything: brightly
colored clothespins on the line, a cross-shaped coral earring whose

46

match is lost, books of fairy tales we read aloud at night.

I must be
dumb as a gunnysack of hammers.

Wind still blows through open
windows like it always used to do.

What did I love that made me
believe it would last?

PUTTING DOWN THE NIGHT

The whole night sky went bad in the knees,
Nothing to pin it up but stars.
I held the whole night sky pinned up with stars
On a short tether and pulled the trigger.
All but a few stars fell in streaks like sudden rain.
That wasn't *supposed* to happen, but then,
What is?
So now the night sky is part of everything.
I did that.
Small and coincidental,
I was still recognizable on my wave of ruin.
The stars that were left I named the constellation *Halter*,
And I carried it in my left hand.
Don't get me wrong.
That wasn't the only night.
There is no end to nights of stars —
Northern light nights, nights skewbald and bay.
And what did all the other nights think
When I led mine away into the woods
Where our footfalls on dry pine needles crackled,
A self-fulfilling prophecy
Of Hell just before it's lit.
I'd like a rainy night right about now.
I'd like a whole remuda of rainy nights
And snowy nights, nights with more stars
Than spaces between stars,
All pressed together against the black gate,
Eyes on the woods,
Where I disappeared with my night sky on her tether.

I'd like to know what they thought,
If nights have thoughts,
When I came out of the woods alone,
Smelling of gunpowder,
A loose halter of stars in my hand
That I hung on a nail
For rain to wash the blood away —
The rain that never rains,
The rain I remember like the long streaks of her forelock
Down over her moss-agate eyes.

SPLINTERS OF THE TRUE CROSS

There are enough splinters of the true cross
To build an ark, those slivers silvering
In reliquary salt. What should we load
The ark with — knucklebones and eyes, charred heads?
Crosses of cartilage from martyrs' hearts,
Archeiropoietos, some blood-dried nails?
And what from nature qualifies as holy?
The ark is rational quite suddenly,
Infinite in reliquary light —
All the world in reliquary light.
If doomsday isn't just another Sunday,
Then launch the ark across the blood-dark sea.
Add a sunset to remember that
You won't be coming back again this way.

NATURE AVERTS HER EYES

Fool. He's mad that trusts in the
tameness of a wolf, a horse's
health, a boy's love, or a whore's
oath.

KING LEAR

Fool. I had an exaggerated interest in death, so much so it was
possible I might already be dead.

Anyway, I had this ridiculous
feeling that I could walk around, that I had found my wallet, that a
beautiful woman had kissed me twice, once on each of the lenses of
my spectacles.

No, that's wrong.

Actually I was someone else.

Could it be you?

Is causality a structure?

Nothing happens that is
supposed to happen, of that I am certain.

Probability cannot be
enthusiastic, only the unlikely can.

Your voice is velvety.

Watch
out.

I have inspected my restored order and find it wanting, insipid
even.

I'm getting drowsy, a good sign.

Yesterday was different.

I
tried to convince myself that passion was not a gyre of dust

swirling about my feet.

Would you like a biscuit?

I lived in a
lukewarm province until it became unbearable.

I touched
everything.

It didn't help.

The room insists.

My categorical
imperative is falling in love.

I saw a ship dancing on waves.

It even
kicked up its heels.

It heeled over.

That ship will never sink alone,
without a captain.

Scientific aspirations, curiously inaccurate,
unrolled before the innocents.

The subject had arisen.

Something
like happiness had long since lost my other.

Dark eyes staring into
ice blue ones.

I do not want to know how old the stars are.

I do not
want to know how long they have left on their astral death row.

As
if they really existed, like gods.

What's their point?

It was very
quiet in the Faculty Club as, outside, the firing squad took aim.

Lightning's alphabet.

Little circles, sightless, float down the river to
the sky.

3

1, 2, 3

This cinquecento hilltop town is like a planet with a dark side and a
deep center.

    If walls are wedding rings (they are) this town has said
I do a lot of times without once meaning it, any more than the
rainbow's end believes that it exists.

    In Todi, here, the outer ring is
oldest, Etruscan, shored up by Roman legions, tuck-pointed by
countless of the nameless cinquecento terrified.

    Uphill through
several circles of walls — more like water ripples than masonry — on
skinny streets haphazard in their ways, I followed my friend
Beppe, a caving fool, toward the center of the town, Piazza del
Popolo, del Duomo, the height of town, planet, history, what you
will.

    He set his rucksack of devices down — the miners' hats and
lights, some bread and wine for when we reemerged, a crowbar and
some climbing rope.

    He levered up a manhole cover in the middle of
the street, pushed out his chin the way Italians do to mean, *who
cares*, and said with a wink, *I'm authorized.*

    Above, the night was
bruisy, starless because of streetlights and people's windows.

Beppe fastened the end of his rope to the frail bumper of a Fiat
Topolino (cinquecento, if you must know — see how numbers never
change?), and dropped the other end into the hole.

    No sound came

back, suggesting that the rope end dangled mid-dark and hadn't
reached (not even close) the end of anything.

What if the owner of
this car drives off for groceries or something?

Beppe seemed
confused.

He shook his head.

Who would drive off in a car tied to a
hole?

We rappelled into the planet.

Our headlights wobbled like the
pointers of senile professors over the omniscient limestone walls
and disappeared into the deeps they were too weak to fathom.

Our
planet had no solid core that we could reach, no center, rather it was
a system of passageways, like an ant farm — waterways, really,
ducts and drains, cisterns and subterranean wells Etruscans
excavated and Romans, in their way, expanded.

The rope's end
swayed halfway down the breach of a lightless well where we
traversed some slimy sideways moves into a waterway.

Cunicoli,
they're called.

You have to put your knees against your chin and
twist sidelong to make your awkward way.

Down in, down in, and
down, and down.

How far is in?

Right here.

We just kept squeezing

58

our inappropriate bodies through the downward ways — the only
ways there were.

Before the Middle Ages, the Piazza del Popolo was
a giant funnel that filled these cisterns (careful) you see here, in case
there was a siege and wells ran dry — wells like this one, as we
stretched across another abyss our lights were too weak to plumb,
though pebbles we dislodged made sure we knew that water waited
there — for what?

Here's the furnace, or one of them.

The ceiling is
so low they must have used dwarfs and child slaves.

They stoked
the fire so hot it melted rock all round.

Here, take this as a souvenir.

He handed me a chunk of annealed conglomerate.

From this hell the
gentry had hot running water and heat in winter from lead pipes
just beneath their floors.

Etruscans had more luxury than we Todini
have.

You think things change?

You think there's progress?

Magari.

Down we went all twisted, double-bent, slathered in the liquid
limestone slime.

I was choking, not from sulfur stink, but
claustrophobia of the underneath of civilization, which is not
civilized, but dank.

Beppe found a Roman coin in the wink of his
miner's lamp, a piece of luck.

I figured I'd got the point and wanted
out.

The farther down we went the farther back it was.

Right now
we are a hundred meters below the Duomo.

Mum, I thought it far
enough.

But Beppe said I had to see the drain.

The drain went down
and so, good God, did we.

Twisted, contorted, like any cinquecento
painter's damned, we stopped at the juncture of crossed *cunicoli.*

You first, my friend and trusted guide said, stepping aside.

You
won't be sorry to have come so far in darkness.

Down and down
and farther down to where a liplike spout came out halfway up
the town's most outer defense, her first false promise, I stepped
into the air and straightened.

All around the cinquecento town, my
dear planet, and all above were fuzzy stars, like nightfires of an
army laid in siege, and all eternity to wait us out.

2

The Simultaneous City

Just take away time and you're here, as surely you remember from
the first visit.
        Nothing starts over and nothing ever ends, or rather,
nothing stops ending.
           It's a city of endings that never ends.
                Am I
being clear?
        Everything just keeps ending.
           Perhaps the city is
misnamed.
        It was as close to the truth as we could come.
           As you
may remember from your first time here, the tour is required.
           Hurry
up, it has already ended.
        But really, there is no hurry.
           Every other
year since nineteen eighty-three I've gone to Roger's Shoes to buy a
pair of new Redwing work boots from Roger.
        To get to Roger's
Shoes I have to pass the same house where I met my ex-and-only-
wife, twenty-six years ago — same house we passed on the way to
the class where they teach you how to get divorced after twenty-six
years together, if you have a daughter.
        It's like the opposite of
Lamaze, where we are still learning how to breathe.

In the delivery
room Lily Tomlin is still on TV, sitting in a giant chair so that she
looks like a little girl.

She is a little girl.

I have a little girl, who is
carefully descending the stairs.

She has to reach over her head for
the banister and she only steps down to the next step with her left
foot: left foot, left foot, left foot.

Her hair is wispy fine and blond
as a dandelion gone to seed and not yet wished upon.

Meanwhile,
she's tripping lightly down the stairs, late for her riding lesson, as
she gracefully descends, a beautiful young woman in an evening
gown, to meet her date at the door, who will be waiting there
forever.

OK, now I'm jogging toward the river, down the same
street I always run, where I walked my little girl (who is away at
college) each morning to Lincoln Elementary School, then on across
the river I keep crossing and recrossing, to get to Roger's Shoes.

I
pass the apartment where Lowell and Hardwick still live, the house
on Bowery where my teacher, Donald Justice, is writing *The
Summer Anniversaries*, and one of my students is committing
suicide — same apartment — letting the sink fill up with blood.

But
Don and Jean still walk, somewhat stooped now, down along the
river, where all I ever wanted was what they have together.

The
leaves are dropping from the ash in my front yard, which isn't the
end of anything.

My wife who never left is gone, my daughter is
coming home for Thanksgiving.

Look, there's Roger's Shoes.

If
you are looking for work boots, Redwings are the best, even if they
cost a little more.

Take it from me, they last forever.

Oh, and one
last unending fact (I'm sure you remember from before): all of us
have already died, the particulars don't matter, even the love of my
unending life, my beautiful daughter, dressed as an angel with
Halloween wings, dressed for a wedding, dressed for a wake, her
innocence unending, her experience without end, waiting at the top
of the stairs.

3

Dear Miss Emily

I knew the end would be gone before I got there.
After all, all rainbows lie for a living.
And as you have insisted, repeatedly,
The difference between death and the *Eternal*
Present is about as far as one
Eyelash from the next, not wished upon.
Rainbows are not forms or stories, are they?
They are not doors ajar so much as far-
Flung situations without true beginnings
Or any ends — why bother — unless, as you
Suggest — repeatedly — there's nothing wrong
With *this* life, and we should all stop whining.
So I shift my focus now on how to end
A letter. In XOXOXO,
For example, Miss, which are the hugs
And which the kisses? Does anybody know?
I could argue either way: the O's
Are circles of embrace, the X is someone
Else's star burning inside your mouth;
Unless the O is a mouth that cannot speak,
Because, you know, it's busy.
X is the crucifixion all embraces
Are, here at the nowhere of the rainbow's end,
Where even light has failed its situation,
Slant the only life it ever had,
Where even the most gallant sunset can't
Hold back for more than a nonce the rain-laden

Eastern sky of night. It's clear. It's clear.
X's are both hugs and kisses, O's
Where stars that died gave out, gave up, gave in —
Where no one meant the promises they made.
Oh, and one more thing. I send my love
However long and far it takes — through light,
Through time, through all the faithlessness of men,

James Augustin Galvin,

His mark.

ABOUT THE AUTHOR

James Galvin was raised in northern Colorado. He has
published five collections of poetry, most recently *Resurrection
Update: Collected Poems, 1975-1997* (Copper Canyon Press, 1997),
which was a finalist for the *Los Angeles Times* Book Award, the
Lenore Marshall Poetry Prize, and the Poets' Prize. He is also
the author of the critically acclaimed prose book *The Meadow*
(Holt, 1992) and a novel, *Fencing the Sky* (Holt, 1999). His
honors include a Lila Wallace-Reader's Digest Foundation
Award, a Lannan Literary Award, and fellowships from the
Guggenheim Foundation, the Ingram Merrill Foundation,
and the National Endowment for the Arts. He has a
home, some land, and some horses outside of Tie Siding,
Wyoming, and he is a member of the permanent faculty
of the University of Iowa Writers' Workshop.

Copper Canyon Press wishes to acknowledge the support of Lannan Foundation in funding the publication and distribution of exceptional literary works.

LANNAN LITERARY SELECTIONS 2003

James Galvin, X
Antonio Machado, *Border of a Dream: Selected Poems of Antonio Machado*,
translated by Willis Barnstone
Antonio Porchia, *Voices*, translated by W.S. Merwin
Rabindranath Tagore, *The Lover of God*, translated by
Tony K. Stewart and Chase Twichell
César Vallejo, *Black Heralds*, translated by Rebecca Seiferle

LANNAN LITERARY SELECTIONS 2002

Cesare Pavese, *Disaffections: Complete Poems 1930-1950*,
translated by Geoffrey Brock
Kenneth Rexroth, *The Complete Poems of Kenneth Rexroth*, edited by
Sam Hamill and Bradford Morrow
Alberto Ríos, *The Smallest Muscle in the Human Body*
Ruth Stone, *In the Next Galaxy*
C.D. Wright, *Steal Away: Selected and New Poems*

LANNAN LITERARY SELECTIONS 2001

Hayden Carruth, *Doctor Jazz*
Norman Dubie, *The Mercy Seat: Collected & New Poems, 1967-2001*
Theodore Roethke, *On Poetry & Craft*
Ann Stanford, *Holding Our Own: The Selected Poems of Ann Stanford*,
edited by Maxine Scates and David Trinidad
Reversible Monuments: Contemporary Mexican Poetry, edited by
Mónica de la Torre and Michael Wiegers

LANNAN LITERARY SELECTIONS 2000

John Balaban, *Spring Essence: The Poetry of Hồ Xuân Hương*
Sascha Feinstein, *Misterioso*
Jim Harrison, *The Shape of the Journey: New and Collected Poems*
Maxine Kumin, *Always Beginning: Essays on a Life in Poetry*
W.S. Merwin, *The First Four Books of Poems*

The Chinese character for poetry
is made up of two parts: "word" and "temple."
It also serves as pressmark for Copper Canyon Press.

Founded in 1972, Copper Canyon Press remains dedicated
to publishing poetry exclusively, from Nobel laureates to new and
emerging authors. The Press thrives with the generous patronage of
readers, writers, booksellers, librarians, teachers, students, and
funders — everyone who shares the conviction that poetry invigorates
the language and sharpens our appreciation of the world.

PUBLISHERS' CIRCLE
The Allen Foundation for the Arts
Lannan Foundation
National Endowment for the Arts

EDITORS' CIRCLE
Thatcher Bailey
The Breneman Jaech Foundation
Cynthia Hartwig and Tom Booster
Target Stores
Emily Warn and Daj Oberg
Washington State Arts Commission

For information and catalogs:
COPPER CANYON PRESS
Post Office Box 271
Port Townsend, Washington 98368
360/385-4925
www.coppercanyonpress.org

The text in this book is set in Adobe Jenson, a historical revival of Nicolas Jenson's fifteenth-century Venetian roman. Jenson has an even and upright appearance, and captures the liveliness of Italian Renaissance writing hands.

Design and composition by Shari DeGraw.

CPSIA information can be obtained
at www.ICGtesting.com
Printed in the USA
LVHW031321281021
701801LV00001B/6

9 781556 591914